BEN WICKS'
BORN TO READ AND COOK

SEARS Canada is committed to supporting the family and all those who strive to provide the **_basics_** that underlie the positive development of our children and youth. We call our community focus the Sears **_Young Futures_** commitment. We are honoured that the fine sponsors below share our commitment, and have partnered with us to ensure this book gets into the hands of all Canadian families with young children.

A special thanks from Canada's children to:

CANADIAN AIRLINES
CIBC WOOD GUNDY
HEALTH CANADA
INDUSTRY CANADA
KRAFT CANADA INC. & KRAFT KITCHENS
LAUBACH LITERACY OF CANADA
MEDIACOM
NATIONAL LITERACY SECRETARIAT
NORANDA
ROTARY CLUBS OF CANADA
SEARS CANADA INC.
ST. JOSEPH PRINTING
TEMBEC INC. & SPRUCE FALLS
WRIGLEY CANADA INC.

Once again, **Born To Read And Cook*** *is dedicated to incredibly devoted teachers - the true heroes in a world that often races by our little ones.*

Canadian Cataloguing in Publication Data
Wicks, Ben, 1926-
Ben Wicks' Born to read and cook

Includes index.
ISBN 1-895651-20-4
1. Education, Primary - Parent participation. 2. Reading
- Parent participation. 3. Language arts. 4. Numeracy.
5. Cookery. I. Title. II. Title: Born to read and cook.
LB1525.W528 1998   649' .58   C98-931700-5
© 1998 by Ben Wicks

Published in 1998 by
Ben Wicks & Associates
449A Jarvis Street
Toronto, ON M4Y 2G8 Canada

* Born To Read And Cook
is a trademark of Ben Wicks
Printed & Bound in Canada

CONTENTS

FOREWORD

CANADA

PRIME MINISTER • PREMIER MINISTRE

by

the Right Honourable Jean Chrétien

Supporting families to give our children a good start in life is one of the most important investments Canada can make in its future. It is all about developing healthy, secure children and preparing them for lifelong learning.

Education and learning have always been important. They have always been key to a better future. To greater opportunity and security. I know first hand.

My father worked as a machinist by day and at odd jobs at night so that my brothers, my sisters and I could go to school. And, my parents never stopped believing that I would have a good future if I developed good learning skills – principal among them being literacy skills -- and got a good education. It is why the Chrétien kids from Shawinigan's working class became a respected physician, a pharmacist, a social worker, nurses, successful business people, an eminent medical researcher, and a prime minister of Canada.

With **Born to Read and Cook**, the fourth volume in the Born to Read series, Ben Wicks once again shares with his readers the joys of reading and learning -- this time contributing an invaluable lesson in nutrition. The National Literacy Secretariat and Health Canada are to be commended for their support of this initiative. Available to 2 million children across Canada, I am certain the impact of **Born to Read and Cook** will be very helpful in improving the lives of Canada's future.

Jean Chrétien

ACKNOWLEDGEMENTS

This year we have decided to explore a new space for learning -- the kitchen. Although reading and writing skills are vital to our children, nothing will equal the importance of parents' bonding with their little ones. This is our reason for **Born To Read And Cook**.

With the help of my incredible assistant, Joanne Dicaire, the project has once again reached a successful conclusion. The National Literacy Secretariat, with Laubach Literacy, helped steer us through the mountains of research material and, now, Health Canada has come on board. The forever supportive Senator Joyce Fairbairn constantly found time to encourage us to move forward. The ministries of education not only gave their blessing, but helped with the distribution of the books.

The success of the Born To Read program has, like all winning efforts, been achieved through the tremendous support of all involved, including the Prime Minister of Canada. This group of dedicated Canadians reached out to ensure that another two million Canadian children will hand this book to their parents.

A special thanks to...

Health   Santé
Canada   Canada

Support from the National Literacy Secretariat was administered by Laubach Literacy of Canada.

INTRODUCTION

It's hard to imagine that four years have passed since we produced the first in the Born To Read series.

Each year, children have raced home with these guide books to help parents steer their children along a path that will lead them into the magic world of words.

Almost eight million little ones have now wandered through a looking glass with their parents and found a spider called Charlotte waiting for them.

The incredible passport known as a book has welcomed new adventurers each year. Little explorers are now able to look back on a time when they first sat on their parent's lap and found a magic page waiting to pull them in.

To this end, the newest of our series may seem far removed from our aims of literacy. Yet it is the perfect match.

Born To Read And Cook hits the bullseye as it strives to encourage you, the parent, and your child to bond in the kitchen.

It's the obvious room in which to prepare a nutritious meal and, in so doing, give your child a sense of achievement.

As you turn the pages, know that what you are doing with your child is a joint venture. Words and measuring, although important in their learning process, will fall short of the main goal. Being close and having fun with your child is the aim of this collection of fun food ideas.

Before we enter the kitchen, let's review important sections from the previous three books.

1 ONCE UPON A TIME

Just fifteen minutes a day with a book brought you and your child closer together than you could ever have imagined.

As your child began to grow, you watched tiny fingers hold onto a chair and make a series of wobbly steps before finally falling to the carpet.

As your child's first teacher, you encourage him or her to explore the world. The walks through the countryside or through the shopping mall give you the opportunity to point out all sorts of incredible things, such as birds, bees and even ants.

Every small child has a strange fascination for these tiny creatures, whose aim in life seems to be to run in and out of holes in the sidewalk or grass.

The first time my children saw these fascinating insects, they wanted to step on them.

Many years later, I overheard my eldest daughter explain that one of her earliest memories was of her dad kneeling down beside her and pointing to an ant on which she was about to step.

"That's a little mother who has been shopping and is now hurrying home to her children to read a story," I had said.

My other daughter mentioned remembering her dad as he rushed around the house waving frantically at a fly that he was trying to shoo out of the house through an open window rather than kill it.

As wild and embarrassing as my actions sound, they were important lessons that each of my children learned at an early age.

These events set in motion a gentleness and concern for others, human or other, that exist to this day.

This proves a point. You may say that you are not a teacher, but you are.

Half of your child's mental ability developed between birth and age four. And guess who was in charge? **You**.

You are your child's first teacher. **You** were the one who taught your child to use the potty. **You** were the one who steered your child from danger and, if your child was amongst the lucky ones, **you** were the one who read your child a story as your child snuggled in bed every night. **You** were the one who encouraged your child to take his or her first uneasy steps.

For many of you, that was yesterday. Now, all too soon, your child is leaving the house for a few hours each day and heading for the arms of another teacher.

This teacher will introduce your little one to other children. With these new friends, your child will find that working together and sharing are important lessons in life.

Does this mean your job is over?

Far from it. The bond that you and your child have needs constant refueling.

There's a room that is just waiting for you and your child to bond and it's full of fun things to do together. But first we need to prepare.

2 THE CRAZY TIME OF THE DAY

There are few hours in the day more stressful than those between the hours of 4:00 pm to 6:00 pm.

It's dinner time and most of us are racing around the house in a mad attempt to settle everyone before the main meal of the day.

The pace of our lives is faster than ever before, especially for parents who are not able to be home from work when their kids arrive. Fear not. We're about to stop to smell the roses.

First of all, we need to prepare for our children's arrival from school.

If you are home, get changed, washed or do whatever that is required to get ready and make you feel more relaxed.

The sounds of excited children's voices are already finding their way into the house. It's time to take a deep breath to get ready.

The tension and stress all too common in many houses are about to take over, but not in our house.

Why? Because the minute everyone walks into the house, everyone gets a hug, even the dog. Just home from work? Reach for that hug when you walk through the door.

Once that's out of the way, it's off with the television, down with the volume of the stereo, and ready to lower the stress and tension that noise helps create.

We're about to carry out one of the most difficult acts of parenting. We're about to LISTEN.

Exciting things have happened to your child. If you ask the right way, your child will tell you all about the day.

If it is his or her first day, don't you want to know the name of the new teacher?

Then ask.

Certainly, if your child is carrying school work, you'll want to see it. So what if it's a drawing with the words 'Mom' or 'Dad' underneath and it looks nothing like you.

Picasso drew heads with both eyes on one side of the face. Look for how much they were sold.

There's only one place for your child's art. This is the greatest museum known to a child, the kitchen fridge. Up it goes, accompanied by sighs of 'ahs' and 'ohs'.

There is one more point before we venture into the kitchen.

Because children have small stomachs and don't eat much at any one time, they need to eat often.

Since dinner time is still a while away, they may be in need of something to eat. They're more likely to be cranky if they're hungry.

What to do? The answer is a simple one, a nice healthy snack.

A small nibbles plate fits the bill. Vegetables and dip, fruit plate or fresh berries, small cheese chunks, dried or sliced meats and crackers are just the trick to hold off a rumbling tummy until the main meal.

These snacks are a particularly good idea for those parents who find that they often arrive home after their children.

If you happen to be the kind of parent who feels that jumping in immediately is particularly stressful, before anyone gets home, take a short, relaxing walk.

Feel better?

Good, then bring out your plate of vegetables and dive in.

There's lots of listening to be done.

3 SHOPPING

There is nothing worse than facing a recipe knowing that you have forgotten a vital ingredient.

This is not going to happen to us. We have a wonderful set of specially prepared recipes with the ingredients clearly bolded for us.

So begin, both you and your child, by taking this book and making a shopping list of the ingredients needed for the meal you have BOTH chosen to prepare.

Making this list together will demonstrate to your child that reading and writing are important. Just one little reminder. This is fun, not a school exam.

Before setting out for the store (or gathering ingredients from your garden), you may be the kind of shopper that saves coupons.

If so, give your child the opportunity to sort them before going out.

Some of the coupons may be for canned goods, milk products, or meats.

Sort them together. Mention what the coupon is for and count together how much money can be saved.

Inside the store.

Have your child hold the list and read off the items. Your little one can even help spot where the items can be found.

If you have coupons, match them with the items on the shelves.

Since this is a fun way for your child to improve his or her reading skills, look together for the items you want in the store.

When you pick an item, read the price together. If your child is old enough to read, by all means, let him or her tell you the price.

Show your child the different ways that foods are measured. Some foods go by weight, with the amounts shown in grams and kilos. Liquids are measured by volume, with the amounts shown in millilitres or litres.

Point to each item or, better yet, pick the item up and show what you are explaining.

The vegetable section is a great area for fun with numbers. Some items may be priced by the dozen. Show how many you can buy for a dollar. Help your child to figure it out and KEEP IT FUN!

One way of doing this is to allow your child to weigh some of the fruits and vegetables. Ask which one weighs the most and see if your child can work out the cost.

Talk about best buys and let your child decide which one you should buy.

The bill.

As you tour the store, add the prices to your list together. Round them off to the nearest dollar to make the numbers easier to count.

Have your child figure out the cost and then give him or her enough money to pay the bill. Point out how much money was given to the cashier and how much change was received.

We have the food we need for a wonderful meal. Now let's get home and get started.

4 INTO THE KITCHEN

It's a magic place, with food and fellowship casting a peculiar spell over a room that retains a wonderful sense of warmth.

For little ones, it is the perfect place to practice their reading, writing and counting while having fun.

We should, however, be aware that these hours of normal stress are the ones most prone to accidents, so make sure the kitchen is a safe place for your child.

Here is a check list to help you.

- Pot handles are turned in and pots are at the back of the stove.

- Items which catch fire easily, such as clothes, paper or books, are not hung or stored near the stove. Hair should be tied back.

- Knives and sharp utensils are out of reach.

- Electrical appliances (toasters, electric fry pans) are away from water and unplugged.

- Cords should not be dangling from electrical appliances.

- A working fire extinguisher is available.

- Always use oven mitts when preparing hot foods.

- Household cleaners and chemicals are stored up high in locked cupboards.

Okay. Everything in order? Good, then.

Away we go!

Preparation.

Make sure that your hands have been washed and that the surfaces and the utensils you are going to use for preparing the food are clean.

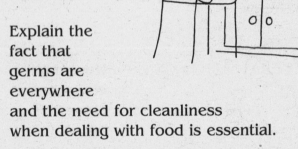

Explain the fact that germs are everywhere and the need for cleanliness when dealing with food is essential.

An apron for everyone (treat it like a kitchen uniform) is also important to keep clothes clean. Helping each other tie the strings at the back can add to the fun and give a sense of doing something special together.

It's going to be the main meal of the day, so get everyone involved in the preparation (except the dog).

Even small children can set tables and so on. Babies too young to help can be placed in a highchair in the kitchen with the family. You'll be surprised how much fun they'll have watching everyone else enjoying themselves.

Remember, this is not just a time to cook; it is a time for the whole family to bond. Your child will have a wonderful opportunity to bond, so get talking.

What recipe to prepare?

That's easy. Just turn the pages of this book and there are plenty of wonderful, quick and easy nutritious meals.

Involve your child in the choice. This is a joint effort and the result will be all the more fun if your child feels that he or she was partly responsible for the meal's success.

By encouraging your child to follow along with the recipe, you'll give him or her a fun way of improving literacy skills.

Once you have chosen one of the recipes in this book, gather the various things you will require. Start cooking when you have everything you need.

It's vital that you work together as you prepare the various cooking ingredients and utensils that are required.

Let your child call out from the list as you listen and set aside what you need. (For your child, it's called reading).

Would you like to add something? Let your child include it in the list. (It's called writing).

Make sure your child includes the right amount of the ingredient that was added. (It's called counting).

Didn't I tell you that cooking with your child would be fun?

Now it's time for the food experts in the Kraft Kitchens to give us a series of recipes that are simple for you and your child to prepare **together**.

With each idea, your child can learn a new skill, like chopping, spreading or measuring.

Try one at a time.

Ready?

Okay. Let's get in that kitchen and start cooking up a storm.

SPEEDY CHEESY BREAKFAST BAGELS
(Breakfast)

Learning: Slicing a bagel, scrambling eggs.

1. Place a **bagel** on a cutting board. Using a bread knife or a knife with a 'jagged' edge, slice bagel in half. Always have Mom or Dad in the kitchen when using sharp objects. Place both halves in toaster and toast until lightly browned. Remove carefully from toaster. They can be really hot. Be very careful.

2. Spread toasted bagel halves with process **cheese** or your favourite cheese.

3. Using a small bowl, such as a cereal bowl, break and beat one **egg** with a fork until well mixed. Place **a little butter, margarine or oil** in the bottom of a frying pan. Heat pan over medium heat. Add egg, cook and stir with a wooden spoon until scrambled (egg should not have any runny or liquid parts in it).

4. Spoon the cooked egg onto the bagel halves and top with additional cheese, if desired.

5. Serve this with a glass of your favourite **juice**.

MY FAVOURITE CEREAL AND TOAST
(Breakfast)

Learning: Do it yourself.

1. The night before, take **your favourite breakfast cereal** out of the cupboard. Pour it into a cereal bowl. Cover with napkin. Then you can eat as soon as you get downstairs without having to wait for Mom or Dad.

2. In the morning, place a piece of **bread** in toaster and toast. Remove from toaster and spread with **peanut butter** and **jam**. Cut into your favourite shapes with Mom's **cookie cutters** or into toast fingers.

3. Pour **milk** onto cereal and eat. Remember to have a good breakfast in the morning because it will help you at school so you don't feel too tired before lunch. And don't forget the **juice** to give you the vitamins and minerals you need to grow big and strong.

PIT STOP SINGLES SANDWICH
(Lunchbox)

Learning: Roll-ups - a different way to make a sandwich.

1. Spread **salad dressing** on a **medium flour tortilla**. Add some **salsa** if you like.

2. Top tortilla with **lettuce**, two slices of your favourite **meat such as ham or bologna** and a slice of **process cheese or cheddar**. Roll the tortilla.

3. Place tortilla on cutting board and carefully cut in half. Wrap tightly in plastic wrap and store in refrigerator overnight.

4. Cut stem end off **carrot**. Carefully peel the carrot. Wash under cold water. Cut into long pieces.

5. For **celery**, wash well under cold water. Cut a little off both ends and trim off any brown spots. Place on cutting board and cut into sticks.

6. If you wish to make the carrot and celery sticks for the entire week, place in a container in the refrigerator in cold water and they will keep for five days.

7. In the morning, pack carrot and celery sticks in a small container. Place in lunchbox along with a **roll up**, **juice** and snacks for a recess treat.

TUNA BUNWICH
(Lunchbox)

Learning: Chopping.

1. Open a can of **tuna** (170 g). Drain off the liquid and place in a mixing bowl. Add 50 mL (1/4 cup) **salad dressing** and mix with a fork. Place two washed **green onions** on a chopping board. Carefully cut into very small pieces. Add these to the tuna. Wash a piece of **celery**. Carefully cut it into small pieces and add to the tuna. Mix the tuna salad well.   (If you don't like green onion, cut half an apple into small pieces and add instead.)

2. Take a couple of leaves of your favourite **lettuce** from the head. Run the lettuce under cold water and wash any sand off of it. Place on paper towel to dry well.

3. With **butter or margarine**, butter both sides of the **bun** (hot dog or ham burger buns make a fun change). Cover the bottom half of the bun with lettuce and then the tuna mixture. Place second half of bun on top. Cover with plastic wrap or place in a sandwich container.

4. Place sandwich in the refrigerator overnight and it will be ready for a delicious lunch the next day. Pack an **apple**, **milk** and a **pudding** snack to make a great lunch. One way to keep sandwiches cool until lunch time is to pack them next to a frozen drink or an ice pack.

WESTERN SANDWICH
(Weekend lunch recipe)

Learning: Microwaving.

1. Heat 15 mL (1 tbsp.) **process cheese spread or grated cheddar** in a dish that can go in the microwave oven for 20 seconds on MEDIUM power.

2. Take **two eggs** out of the refrigerator. Using a small bowl, break and beat eggs, add cheese and stir until mixed. For added flavour, chop up one washed **green onion** and add to egg.

4. Put bowl back into the microwave oven and cook on MEDIUM power for one minute. Open microwave door and carefully stir. Cook another minute on MEDIUM power.

5. Toast two slices of **bread** and spread with process cheese spread. Place egg mixture between bread slices. Cut into triangles. This sandwich is great with **milk** and **peanut butter cookies** for dessert.

MINI-PITA PIZZA
(Weekend lunch)

Learning: Broiling.

1. Using a thin knife, split a **pita** in half. Toast in a toaster oven or under a pre-heated broiler until lightly browned.

2. Place a **can of pasta sauce** (your favourite kind) on the counter. With a can opener, carefully remove lid from surface of cleaned can, being very careful, as it is very sharp.

3. Using a spoon, spread pita halves with pasta sauce. Top pita halves with **process cheese slices or grated cheddar**.

4. On a cutting board, carefully slice your **favourite toppings, such as hot dog, ham, mushroom or green pepper**. Place on top of cheese.

5. Place pizzas back in toaster oven and toast for five minutes, or until cheese melts, or place in the oven and broil until cheese melts. These will be great served with your favourite kind of **yogurt** and **juice or milk**.

THE BEST-GRILLED CHEESE SANDWICH
(Weekend lunch)

Learning: Frying and flipping.

1. Choose two slices of your favourite **bread**.
Place on a cutting board.

2. Spread bread slices (both sides of each slice)
with **butter or margarine**.

3. Place one or two pieces of **process cheese or
sliced cheddar** between bread.

4. Place a frying pan on top of stove burner. Turn
burner onto medium heat. Carefully place sandwich
on bottom of pan.

5. Cook until lightly browned on the bottom. Using
a lifter, carefully turn sandwich over and cook on
the other side until cheese melts and bread is
browned.

Using spatula, remove
sandwich from pan and
place on cutting board.
Cut and place on plate.

This tastes great with
veggies and **salad
dressing** as a
dip and your
favourite
fruit
juice
to
drink.

BEAR PAWS
(After school snack)

Learning: Peeling.

1. Using **round crackers** or **small rice cakes**, spread with **process cheese spread** or top with **cheddar cheese** and melt in microwave on medium setting.

2. Peel **carrots**. Using a cutting board and a sharp knife, carefully slice carrots into small rounds.

3. Place a carrot round on each snack.

4. Place **raisins** on each snack to resemble a bear's paw.

Eat and have fun.

NACHOS
(Anytime snack or light dinner)

Learning: Baking.

1. Turn oven on to 200°C (400°F).

2. Place one bag (200 g) **tortilla chips** in a large baking dish that can go in the oven.

3. Sprinkle chips with one package (200 g) **shredded cheese**. On a cutting board, chop two **green onions** and one **tomato** into small pieces. Sprinkle onion and tomato evenly over surface of chips.

4. Wearing oven mitts, carefully open oven door and place dish on middle oven rack. Bake for eight to ten minutes or until cheese is just melted. Remove from the oven with oven mitts and place on a heat-proof surface. Serve this with **sour cream** and **salsa** if you like.

CRISPY 15 MINUTE CHICKEN NUGGETS
(Dinner)

Learning: Handling chicken.

1. Heat oven to 200°C (400°F). Line a shallow baking pan with foil. Empty one pouch **coating mix** for chicken into shaker bag.

2. Using a cutting board, cut four boneless **chicken breasts** into six to seven nuggets each (try to keep nuggets the same size).

3. Moisten chicken pieces with water. Shake four or five pieces at a time in bag. Place on foil-lined pan. Wash your hands well with an anti-bacterial soap after cutting chicken to be sure you don't spread any germs in the kitchen. Raw chicken sometimes can have germs that are killed when the chicken is cooked. This is called Salmonella and can make you very sick, so be 'chicken wise'. Also be sure to clean your counter, or anywhere else raw chicken juices have been, with a disinfectant.

4. Place chicken in hot oven and bake for ten minutes or until chicken pieces are no longer pink in the middle. With oven mitts, remove pan from oven. Serve nuggets and **fresh vegetables** with your favourite **dip**.

Ice cream would go well for dessert.

FAVOURITE MACARONI AND CHEESE
(Dinner)

Learning: Boiling water.

1. Measure 1.5 L (six cups) **water** into a large pot. Add 5 mL (one tsp.) **salt**. Place on top of stove burner. Turn element onto high heat. When water is boiling, add dry **macaroni noodles** (from a 225 g boxed dinner mix). Stir with a large spoon. Be careful around the stove.

2. Keep boiling the macaroni noodles for about six to eight minutes or until they are cooked the way you like. Turn off element and remove pot.

3. Place a large colander in the sink. Bring pot to sink and pour into colander to drain off water.

4. Place cooked macaroni back in pot and add 45 mL (three tbsp.) **butter or margarine** and 40 mL (1/4 cup) **milk** and the **cheese sauce mix**. Stir well.

5. You can add a lot of your favourite things to this macaroni dinner, such as a can of drained **tuna**, cut up **hot dogs**, drained canned **vegetables**. Experiment and come up with your own creation!! This dinner would be great with Berry Black Bee Dessert (see recipe page 43) and **juice or milk.**

FIESTA FAJITAS
(Dinner)

Learning: Stir frying.

1. Cut one **onion** and one **green pepper** into strips on a cutting board. Cut 250 g (1/2 lb) **mushrooms** into slices.

2. Add a little **oil** to a frying pan. Place over medium heat, cook and stir the vegetables for about three minutes. Remove from heat.

3. Add 250 mL (one cup) of your favourite **salsa** and 375 mL (1-1/2 cups) **shredded cheese** to the vegetables.

4. Warm **tortillas** in oven or in microwave according to the directions on the package. Place one tortilla on each dinner plate. Spoon mixture into centre of each of four tortillas. Top with shredded **lettuce** and chopped **tomato**, if you wish.

5. Starting at the bottom of the tortilla, fold bottom third up towards top of tortilla. Now roll tortilla from left to right until filling is enclosed. Eat right away. These would be great with your favourite **juice or milk** and **pudding** for dessert.

SOUP WITH CHEESE CROUTONS
(Weekend lunch)

Learning: Broiling.

1. Make your favourite homemade **vegetable soup** or heat up a can of your favourite soup.

2. Toast enough slices of **French bread** so that each person has one. Place the slices on a shallow baking sheet.

3. Top each slice of bread with your favourite kind of **grated cheese**, such as cheddar or mozzarella (or even a combination of both).

4. Place pan about 15 cm (six inches) from the top broiler element. Turn on broiler.

5. Watch carefully and broil only until the cheese is melted. Remove from oven with oven mitts. Turn off broiler.

6. Place one crouton on top of each bowl of soup. Enjoy!! This soup would be great with **milk** and **yogurt** for dessert.

ONE POT CHEESY PASTA
(Dinner)

Learning: Handling and cooking ground beef.

1. Place 500 g (one lb) **lean ground beef** in a large frying pan. Turn stove top element onto medium heat and cook meat until there is no pink colour left, stirring occasionally. If you touch the raw meat with your hands, be sure to wash hands well. Don't forget to clean off surfaces with a disinfectant if any raw juices from the meat have leaked out of the package.

2. Place a colander in the sink and carefully drain the fat from the meat. Cook your favourite shape of **pasta**, drain and measure 1.25 L (five cups). In the large frying pan, add the pasta to the cooked ground beef along with one jar (750 ml) of **pasta sauce** and 125 mL (1/5 cup) **parmesan cheese**. Mix until well combined.

3. Sprinkle the top of the pasta with 500 mL (two cups) **shredded cheese**. Turn the heat to low, cover, and heat until cheese is melted and sauce is bubbly.

4. Spoon onto dinner plates.

This would taste great with a **fresh fruit cup** for dessert and **juice or milk**.

NO FLOUR PEANUT BUTTER COOKIES

Learning: Measuring dry ingredients.

1. Get out your parents' set of measuring cups for measuring dry ingredients. These are cups that should always be used to measure flour, sugar, and chocolate chips - anything that is dry, not wet. Remember to level off with a knife.   This will give you accurate measures when baking and will ensure success!! If you don't have these measures, ask Mom or Dad if they can buy you some. They aren't expensive and you will be able to bake lots of goodies for your family with them!

2. Spoon **peanut butte**r into a 250 mL (or one cup) measure, pushing down to make sure you fill up all the spaces. When its full, level off with a knife. Spoon measured peanut butter into a large bowl.

3. Measure the **sugar** in the same way as the peanut butter, spooning into a 250 mL (or one cup) measure and levelling off with a knife. Pour into the mixing bowl.

4. Add one **egg** and mix until all the ingredients are well combined. Stir in 250 mL (or one cup) **chocolate chips**.

5. Form dough into 2.5 cm (one-inch) balls. Place on shallow baking pan. Press down lightly with a fork. Bake at 180°C (350°F) for 10 to 12 minutes or until lightly browned. Remove with oven mitts and cool on wire rack. Makes about three dozen cookies.

BERRY BLACK BEE DESSERT

Learning: Measuring liquids.

1. Place **water** in kettle and boil. Carefully pour water into a glass measuring cup and measure 250 mL (or one cup). To check for accuracy, look at the water at eye level to be sure you have the correct amount. This glass measuring cup should be used for measuring all liquid ingredients when cooking such as water, oil, juice, milk.

2. Place one package (85 g) **black jelly powder** in a bowl. Add boiling water and stir until powder is dissolved, about two minutes. Stir in 125 mL (1/2 cup) **cold water**.

3. Pour jelly into a nine-inch (2.5 L) square pan and chill for about one hour.

4. When the jelly is set, prepare one package (four-serving size) **vanilla instant pudding** according to the directions on the package, reducing the **milk** to 375 mL (1-1/2 cups).

5. To make the bees, break the jelly with a fork. Alternately, layer jelly and pudding in five clear dishes, ending with pudding layer.

6. Decorate each bee with two **chocolate wafer cookies** for wings, one **black jelly candy** for a head and two pieces of **black shoestring licorice** for antennae. This will make five bees.

PUDDING CUP CONES

Learning: Stirring.

1. Prepare one package (4-serving size) **instant pudding** (your favourite flavour), as directed on package. For easy mixing of the powder and the **milk**, use a whisk, and gently stir with the whisk until the powder is blended and the pudding begins to thicken - let stand five minutes.

2. Spoon your favourite flavour of **ice cream** into the bottom of as many **ice cream cones** as you wish.

3. Spoon pudding on top of ice cream. Top with **sprinkles** and serve right away or place back in the freezer and freeze pudding for about one hour if you like.

5 NUTRITION

That was fun but it's time to carry on.

What the
body needs
is not always
what it gets.

So what do
our children
need to keep
up their
energy and
grow into
healthy,
young adults?

Nutritious food.

This is not just for dinner. With every meal, we need to make sure that children are getting a balanced meal.

Where to find protein.

Meat, fish, chicken, milk and cheese are rich in protein, in addition to beans, peas, nuts and seeds.

Where to find iron.

Meat, poultry, fish, breakfast cereals, legumes and dark green vegetables contain iron.

For occasional treats.

Candy, cookies and snack foods like potato chips are to be eaten sparingly.

A little cocoa, chocolate, tea and cola drinks are fine. Just don't overdo the intake.

Allergies.

Some children have them - food that the body rejects.

Please check with your doctor if you feel that certain foods cause a reaction.

Starting the day.

For many families, breakfast is the only time of the day when everyone is home at the same time. It's no wonder that many find it the most important time of the day.

Some may say that they have little time in the morning. **Make time.** It's not difficult to do. There's always the night before to prepare. The benefits are tremendous. You'll find that special morning time will strengthen your family bonds and set a wonderful example for your kids.

Breakfast is a time to refill a body that has been without food for a whole night of sleep. In fact, the word breakfast means what it says. It's a break from fast.

Don't skip on breakfast.

Without this important meal, kids will miss
the nutrients they need. How else will they
be able to learn and stay mentally alert
during their day? Many teachers have seen
that children who skip breakfast are often
inattentive and learn poorly.

So teach your children good eating habits
by starting with a good breakfast and
following through with healthy foods
throughout the day.

For **breakfast**, there are at least three food
groups to choose from - fruit, grains and
milk products. Make sure that the brands
of cereal meet your standards, then let
your child choose.

A simple nutritious **lunch** to prepare is a sandwich, apple and a drink. What do you put in the sandwich? How about some meat, chicken, fish or cheese, together with some milk?

Don't forget fruit. An apple is perfect. Just remember that it is normal when a child decides what was loved yesterday in the sandwich is not what is wanted today.

Finish the day with a balanced **dinner**. As much as possible, include foods from the main food groups; milk products, meat, grains and fruit and vegetables.

Another important note is that if your child is not hungry, do not force your child to eat. Should you notice serious changes in your child's eating habits, however, consult your doctor.

6 HEALTHY EATING

Although some adults find themselves unable to lose weight for various reasons, others can trace the problem back to when they were children.

An overloving parent who constantly feeds his or her child food may be steering this child toward potential health concerns with weight.

Certainly, a child needs to feel full when leaving the table. There is, however, another factor involved. Time.

The family that makes a habit of sitting down to a meal and eating slowly will find that their children will understand the difference between being hungry and feeling full.

It's true that our hectic shedules are far different from those living in the time of

"Little House On The Prairie".

In those times, it seemed that all families counted their meal times as the most important part of the day.

Although we would like things to remain as they were then, life has changed. This is not to say that we cannot adopt some of the more important habits of the past.

How about breakfast together? Or try to at least have a family dinner once a week. Spending time with your children should be shared by all. What better way to monitor your children's eating habits?

Maybe it's time to get out the basketball and throw some hoops.

7 FEEDING THE MONSTER IN THE HOUSE

Although this book concerns itself with bonding in the kitchen, it would not be complete without the mention of 'that monster in the corner'.

What has this to do with cooking? Like preparing meals together, it has everything to do with spending time together.

Should we turn off the television? How harmful is it to our children? Would we be better off throwing it out the window?

Certainly, those children who sit in front of the television set hour after hour will find themselves way behind those children whose parents have the set under control.

How do we do this?

We use it. Without question, television offers many benefits, such as education, entertainment and relaxation.

Let us try to answer the two major concerns for most parents. How much television should our children watch and what are they watching?

Watch the television with them. Cry with them. Laugh with them. Enjoy it as much as they do.

Talk about the program. There are many things that happen on television that are not a true reflection of the real world.

It may help to fill in the gaps for your child by explaining what they have seen to give them a broader and more balanced view.

Little ones can be encouraged to take the next step. How about a visit to the library?

Who said television was a monster?

I did, but it's a monster that can be brought under control.

It just needs to be fed the right amount of viewing food to make the whole family happy.

CONCLUSION

We live in a world that is
moving at such an
incredible rate that it
is difficult for most
of us to keep up.

Surrounded by
constant
attempts to
capture
our
time,
we are
ready to
turn from
the most
precious
being in our
life.

Meanwhile, others feel that to work those
extra hours will bring luxuries to a home
that is missing the one luxury a child
needs - the love and nearness of a parent.

Whether the parent is single or there are
two, the need remains the same.

loved and **shown** that

been planned with
ou to bond with
...en, there are other
...at outdoors, to be

...ere's a baseball game, a ballet, a school play, camping, a soccer game, a hockey game or a hundred other events. Go. Be seen by your child cheering from the sidelines.

You can't bond if you can't find the time to be together with your children. Be there for them. They deserve it.

SEARS*

Sears Canada is honoured that so many fine sponsors decided to partner with us in our *Young Futures* commitment to ensure that **Born To Read And Cook** gets into the hands of all Canadian families with young children.

Together with literacy skills, nutritious foods are vital if our children are to grow into healthy adults. For this reason, it is our sincere wish that you and your child enjoy this wonderful gift from Ben Wicks.

Reading, writing and counting... the perfect recipe for a child's future success. The CIBC Wood Gundy Children's Miracle is a proud partner of the **Born to Read and Cook** program, which makes learning and literacy fun for both children and their parents.

Industry Canada's SchoolNet is a fun learning place on the internet that is helping kids develop the skills they need to communicate effectively in a wired world.

The Computers for Schools program redirects surplus government and business computers to schools and libraries. For more information call 1-800-268-6608.

WWW.SCHOOLNET.CA

There is an important connection between good nutrition and a child's ability to learn. That's why Kraft Canada is proud to be a partner in **Born to Read and Cook**.

Together, children and parents can have fun reading while learning about food and nutrition. This learning opportunity combines food for the body with food for the mind to introduce good food habits for life.

Let's Make Something Good:

Laubach Literacy of Canada (LLC) provides community-based solutions to Canada's literacy needs.

10,000 trained volunteers provide tutoring through Laubach programs at the grass-roots level.

Laubach Literacy of Canada is proud to be part of a project that reinforces the importance of creating a learning culture in the home.

MEDIACOM

As Canada's leading outdoor advertising company, Mediacom makes every effort to support the communities in which we operate.

By giving back to the community, we hope to help improve the quality of life for Canadians and to address some of our most pressing challenges, such as illiteracy.

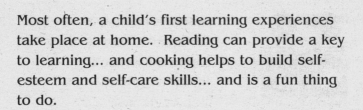

Most often, a child's first learning experiences take place at home. Reading can provide a key to learning... and cooking helps to build self-esteem and self-care skills... and is a fun thing to do.

Noranda is proud to be a part of "Born to Read and Cook". We believe that a successful start to the learning process will ensure a brighter future for all Canadians.

noranda

SEEING THE
FOREST FOR
THE TREES

St. Joseph Printing is very proud to participate in **"Born To Read And Cook"**. We are also pleased that this important literacy program is part of our *Partners In Growth Program*.

To date, under our exclusive reforestation program, we have planted in excess of 560,000 trees in Canada and our goal is to plant two million by the year 2000.

In 1998, Tembec celebrates its 25th anniversary, marking an important milestone in our growth.

We are proud to participate in **"Born To Read And Cook"** to encourage young Canadians to develop the tools of literacy, which will help them reach the important milestones of their lives.

" The more that you read,
the more things that you'll know.
The more that you learn,
the more places you'll go!"

by Dr. Seuss

Wrigley Canada Inc. & **Hubba Bubba** are
proud to support:
Born To Read And Cook.

**This year, we wanted to
share with families a wonderful
place to bond - the kitchen.**

**We hope you have enjoyed this book
and the many adventures in the
years to come, as you learn together
and cook together.**

**Ben Wicks
and the staff at
BORN TO READ**

EMERGENCY NUMBERS

Doctor

_____

Hospital

_____

Poison Control

_____

Ambulance

_____

Police

_____

Fire Department

_____

Neighbour

_____

Relative

_____

Work Numbers

_____

_____